MOMMY'S HAVING TWINS!
A book for the big brother

Jennifer Nevadomski
Juliana D'Alessio

MOMMY'S HAVING TWINS
A book for the big brother

Copyright 2008 by Jennifer Nevadomski and Mommy's Links

All rights reserved. No part of this book may be reproduced or copied without written permission of the author.

This book belongs to

_____

who is the proud big brother to

_____ and _____

I wished for a little sister or brother
and my wish came doubly true!
Instead of having just one baby,
my Mommy's having two!

Mommy's getting very tired.
Their birth day's not far away.
Daddy's getting everything ready.
Can't they be born today?

Things at home will be different.
The babies will cry and
want to play with my toys.
But now I will have two friends
to play with!
I'll just have to get used to their noise!

I am a big brother! The babies are here!
I just got Daddy's call.
I'm going to see Mommy and our babies!
They are so cute but they are so small!

The babies are home now
and I have the best job by far.
I am going to teach them all I know.
Mommy says as a helper, I am her
STAR!

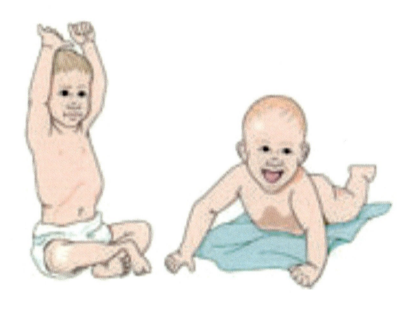

I love to help feed the babies
I rock them to sleep when they nap.
I really think they like to play,
they love it when I dance and clap!

Mommy and Daddy say be careful,
the babies are not as strong as I am yet.
I cannot pick them up without an adult.
But they'll stand up soon on their own,
I bet!

I love being a big brother,
and the twins love me!
We have so much fun together.
We are a special family!

Waiting for MY BROTHERS!

By:
Juliana D'Alessio
July 7, 2008

Juliana drew this picture of her and her Mommy right before the twins were born!

Jennifer Nevadomski, M.S. is a family counselor. After a bumpy road, she welcomed her daughter, Juliana into the world in 2002. Jennifer went on to get her Masters of Science in counseling with an advanced certificate in Marriage and Family Therapy.

In 2005, Jennifer divorced Juliana's father. In 2007, she married Paul Nevadomski, who had a 17 year old son Paulie. After dealing with infertility, the couple welcomed twin boys into their family. Juliana is thrilled to be a big sister to her twin brothers!

Jennifer and Juliana…
Mommy was 8 months pregnant with the twins!

Jennifer has other published works including

BECOMING A MOTHER: Ectopic Pregnancy, Miscarriage, Infertility, Relationships, and My Bumpy Road to Motherhood and OUR TWINS' JOURNAL. For more information, see her storefront at http://stores.lulu.com/store.php?fAcctID=41218 or their website www.mommyslinks.com .

A PICTURE OF ME AND THE TWINS!